Now I Sing

Praise for *Now I Sing*

"Loraine shares deeply personal events of her life, one text at a time, with flamboyant elegance. Even though some of her poems narrate episodes of grief, she manages to captivate the essence of humanity in those moments. Shifting through opposing themes of calmness and anxiety, young and old, hope and fear, family and isolation, there is a thread of survival and celebration that weaves through the whole arc. These poems take-off from where her inaugural anthology, *I Was Not Born a Sad Poet*, left."

Allan Njanji
Researcher in Forced Migration and Refugee Studies

"Loraine's poetry is a physical testimony to her indomitable humanity. Her determination, in practice, to externalise her pain and her joy offers a beautiful inspiration for every one of us to find such a way ourselves and, thereby, share, grow and organise—together—to stop the world's, and each other's, pain and feed our capacities for joy. Free Palestine—Everywhere…"

Dr. Rhetta Moran
Praxivist, writer, mother of three, lifelong learner, RAPAR member

"A brilliant representation of the diaspora way of living. It highlights and raises awareness of the pain and suffering in fighting and navigating the system."

Grace Manyika

Advocate for rights and responsibilities of the African diaspora

"Loraine Mponela is a national treasure."

Tom Green

Senior Producer at Counterpoints Arts

For my only beloved son, Wawishe Sekuzane,
Mr. Humphreys Comfort Mponela

Now I Sing

50 poems to celebrate 50 years

Loraine Masiya Mponela

Cllr Sue
I hope you enjoy the poems!
Thank you for being such
an inspiration!

20th April 2024, London.

published by Kindle Direct Publishing 2024

Published with the assistance of Lou Sarabadzic

ISBN: 9798873747757

CONTENTS

"Loraine has had many challenges over the years but she has used them to improve her life and to help others. She has been strong and resilient in every situation that came her way in caring for family, friends and herself. I wish her all the good she wishes for herself as we mark her 50th birthday. Thank you Loraine."

Joan Proctor

About the author

Loraine Masiya Mponela is an award-winning author, a public speaker, caring mother and warm grandmother. She was born and raised in Malawi and she currently lives in Coventry as a refugee. She was Chair of the Coventry Asylum and Refugee Action Group (CARAG) between 2018 and 2022.

Loraine dedicates most, if not all, of her free time to writing and helping those caught up in the asylum system to rebuild their lives.

Her debut poetry book, *I Was Not Born a Sad Poet*, was published in 2022. This is her second book.

To visit her blog, go to: www.noaudienceloraine.co.uk.

Foreword by Dr. Sue Conlan

Poetry has a unique way of speaking to the heart and to the soul. Loraine's new collection of poetry, *Now I Sing*, does just that. It follows in the footsteps of her first collection, *I Was Not Born a Sad Poet*. It is just as painful, provocative and demanding, drawing as it does on her 50 years of life. In her poems, we sense the common humanity that she calls us to witness and honour, and her strategic role in striving to achieve recognition of that.

Creating from her own experience, Loraine sets out the reality of struggling for acceptance, for peace and justice, not solely for herself but equally, if not more so, for others. In doing so, she is a voice for those who cannot find the words or the strength to speak out. Her poems take us to and bring us back from Malawi, locating her current reality in the context of what she learnt and felt when she was younger. She is present there in thought even if she is not able to be there in person. It is part of who she is.

Loraine takes us to the people who have guided, informed and stood alongside her, drawing on the wisdom of her elders in Malawi. She uses their strength to name the oppression that she and others have faced in the UK. She requires us to feel the pain that has come from humiliation and rejection.

In her poem "Failed," she calls out the use of language which strips people of their humanity and relocates the responsibility where it rightly belongs:

> "we are hurt daily / by words from the powerful
> and the press / words like 'failed' asylum seeker
> is this an examination / in which some pass
> and some don't? / the correct word should be
> *refused* asylum seeker / failed by a hostile system"

Loraine challenges complacency. In "I Was Not Born an Activist," she writes:

> "there isn't one perfect single way
> of being an activist
>
> it is not a vocation
> or a calling
> but the primal human response
> of anger and outrage
> at the injustices being meted out
> on other people
> and the environment"

For myself, the poem *Ubuntu* best encapsulates what motivates Loraine and prevents her from stepping aside from her activism:

> "Ubuntu
> is who I am
> and
> there is no I
> without we"

Loraine's fight is not over, although she needs to make up for the time that she has lost with her son, to get to know and feel the beauty of a relationship with her grandchild. The reality is that not only does Loraine know that she will continue to fight, but we also need her.

In the world in which we live, there isn't an option to be a bystander and simply watch whilst those around us are living through pain that is too often deliberately inflicted by others. We all need to be activists in some shape, form or fashion. Loraine's collection is a call to activism and it helps us to find a way to make a difference. Her life has demonstrated the power of both words and action in working for our common humanity. I am grateful that we have Loraine to stand for us and alongside us. I hope that her words can help heal the wounds of those who, like her, have been failed, and motivate all of us to struggle for a more beautiful world.

Dr. Sue Conlan
December 2023

Sue Conlan is an immigration practitioner and trainer, specialising in supporting people who are in the UK illegally. She is the Director of TACTIC Immigration and Asylum CIC.

Introduction by Aliya Yule

I have had the honour of organising with Loraine in her work as chair of Coventry Asylum and Refugee Action Group (CARAG); I have learnt from Loraine the teacher as she shares her wisdom in how to build power and support refused asylum seekers and migrant communities; and I have been inspired by Loraine the writer who inspires others through her poetry and storytelling.

All of this wisdom - and so much more - is captured in this magnificent collection of Loraine's poetry. The poems span themes including capitalism, imperialism, borders, protest, activism, home, politics, family, racism, community, friendship, ageing, grief, love, joy, longing: the complex experiences that make up the contours of our lives are deeply entwined and profoundly felt in this collection.

Many of her poems shed light on the realities of the violence, brutality and racism of borders, a stark account of life lived under the Hostile Environment immigration system in Britain and under global racial capitalism. From "Keeping Africa Poor" to "We Are Dying," Loraine lays out the scale, depth and sometimes despair of the challenges of the current political moment—which, since she first started writing poetry, have become even greater, with the introduction of several new hostile Immigration Acts of Parliament, the latest Rwanda deportation plan, the expansion of police and state powers to criminalise our communities, and a growing cost of living crisis. Loraine does not shy away from telling her and her community's truth living under such conditions.

But in this context, Loraine offers us many lessons for how we might rise to meet this moment too. "Things to Do When Facing Change" sets out important instructions to organisers and activists: "Allow enough time. Digest and absorb." Many more of these poems are guides from Loraine's life of experience in how we build, connect and continue our long struggles for justice. The poem "Have You?" is a beautiful and heartbreaking call to show up and care for each other: "spread the love / create magic in the hearts of those drowning."

These poems are as much a practice in hope, in building community, in learning to heal and overcome, and to work in solidarity. In "Now I Sing," one of my favourite poems from the whole collection, Loraine reminds us of the necessity and urgency of our collective struggle:

> "let it not be forgotten
> that many still suffer
> with lives in limbo
> this fight has come to an end
> and begun again
>
> see y'all in your streets"

This anthology is a journey of hope, resilience, community and care, and most importantly, of Loraine's remarkable life. I was left with the following lines from "Dear Elder

Loraine," thinking of how lucky we are at Migrants Organise to work with Loraine, and how much she brings to CARAG, to the Solidarity Knows No Borders community, and to everyone lucky enough to meet her:

"all these beautiful beings
pointing to you
as their source"

Aliya Yule, Migrants Organise, 2023

Aliya has worked at Migrants Organise since 2019, and her work currently focuses on the Patients Not Passports campaign. She works with migrant communities and healthcare workers to build opposition to Hostile Environment bordering policies in the NHS, and has developed a direct-action casework model to support individuals excluded from or charged for healthcare to take action. She also works with the Solidarity Knows No Borders network, a community of migrant organisations, groups and individuals, working in solidarity across Britain to organise and build power to end hostility and racism against migrants and refugees.

PART 1

BE

with an introduction
by Laura Nyahuye

Introduction

Be, being, a simple word.

However, it is rather complicated to be in this "be."

It was a general consensus that, to raise a child, it takes a village, in the Zimbabwe I was born into. Growing up, I remember being surrounded by a deep sense of togetherness, "mushandirapamwe." "Ubuntu" is another term that is generally used in the South African continent, a Bantu term meaning "humanity." It's sometimes translated as "I am because we are" (also "I am because you are"), or "humanity towards others."

I believe we are living in such a monumental time in history. The world is becoming smaller, technology is rapidly developing as if its only intention is to outdo humans. Social media is telling us how to dress, eat, start up businesses. If a shooting takes place in California, it is streamed online, in real time. We witnessed George Floyd being murdered in real time. The globe is at the tip of our fingers, with one click we are in Syria, Uganda, China, you name it.

What am I saying here?

I'm talking about identity, being, authentic self. We are in a crisis, yet we are living in one of the most powerful times. A time in history when more than ever, we need to guard our authentic voice. Guard the WHO in us, versus the

WHO in the systematic narrative—the skewered system that sees through colonial, imperial and capitalist lenses. This book is about the "be" in Loraine, yet it is speaking to the "be" in us as humans.

When l reflect on Loraine's journey, I'm struck by how she has managed to live her life, loving fellow humans with a love that's infused with bravery, tenacity and resilience. I wonder how she has created this recipe for life, who gave it to her? Is it her grandmother, is it her people, her village in Karonga in Malawi? In her, l see her grandmother, that l have never met, a grandmother who is long gone, l see her son, a son she longs to see again. I see a fighter, who has managed and continues to navigate a hostile system, for her and for others.

In this section of the book, we get to be intimate with Loraine the mother, the granddaughter, the activist, the friend, the asylum seeker and refugee. What a way to celebrate your 50th birthday, Loraine. Thank you for guarding your authentic voice in a world that is riddled with inhumane acts and violent voices. What a gift you have given us on your 50th birthday!

Laura Nyahuye

Laura Nyahuye is a Senior cultural sector leader, the Creative Director at Maokwo, and an artist.
Having migrated to the UK from Zimbabwe over 20 years ago, Laura has direct lived experience of navigating the UK immigration system and confronting the challenges and

barriers that migrants in our society face everyday. In 2018, she set up Maokwo, dedicated to driving social justice for migrant communities on a regional and national scale, designing and leading change-making interventions across the immigration, voluntary and culture sector. As a practising artist, cultural leader, advocate and activist, Laura convenes, holds and facilitates spaces for deep listening, dialogue and strategic action and has led large-scale commissions and consultancies to promote and embed equity, radical inclusion and systems-change thinking at the level of individuals, community groups, movements and organisations.

Revolution

I rode this horse
I didn't need to ride
but just had to
if sitting on a gigantic creature
walking around the city centre streets
standing at attention position
side by side
facing the cathedral ruins
is what it takes
to bring in change

I rode on a horse to shout out
loud
some people are more equal than others
some people's lives matter more than others

so this white and blue mug
and the black pen
that came with it
placed on the corner of my bedside table
are reminders
that I am here
not just for myself
but to demand

a revolution

Stranger Friend

Lauren Dearest,
I am glad you are my friend

I
who was born in the burning summer
of the African sun
know
you
an English girl
born under the cold snow

I
who hadn't experienced winters
until I was thirty-four
and
you
who have played with snowballs
for as long as you can remember

are joined
in the same name
spelt differently
pronounced the same

I am so grateful
you are my stranger friend
in this land

in which I have lived so many
distasteful moments
and treatments

you stood with me
sharing the aches and pains of life
teaching me
that life challenges us all

without words
you taught me to forgive
those who maybe are victims too
hence they victimise me

I learnt to love a stranger
and voice my innermost feelings
of pain and struggle

you offered an ear to listen
never judging
me, a stranger

my friend
I indeed am grateful
for the messages
and poems we have shared

I read them
again and again
laughing and crying

at different times
realising that
at the bottom of it all
it doesn't take much
to be HUMAN

that's the lesson for me
thank you for sharing your humanity
with such ease

you are a sister
I shall treasure always

yours sincerely,

Loraine.

Keep Busy

one of the ways
one keeps themselves sane
in this hostile environment is
to keep busy

a case in point
      I attend vigils
      I give talks of encouragement
      I scooped my second GCSEs
      at Coventry City College
      and won lecturers' hearts for the Most Focused
      Student award
      I walked in the corridors
      of London College of Communication
      and saw my name
      in the *Guardian Foundation* Newspaper
      as an author
      and have performed at international festivals

you don't have to be better off
to give
just your care
attention and a smile
can heal someone
who is going through a rough patch

get involved in community
activism and activities

there is so much one can get
and give at the same time
and when the mind is not idle
evil and desperate thoughts have no space

Failed

we laugh / we cry
we get anxious sometimes / angry too
in life / we want absolutely nothing
outside the ordinary / only a place
where we can be seen / as human beings
our drives / hopes and fears
are no different / from anybody else's
we want the bare minimum / that makes us all human

we are hurt daily / by words from the powerful
and the press / words like "failed" asylum seeker
is this an examination / in which some pass
and some don't? / the correct word should be
refused asylum seeker / failed by a hostile system

we are people / denied the right
to be human / we are a "swarm of refugees"
as we were / graciously described
by a former Prime Minister / we are
the "filthy other / and pathetic subspecies"
in the eyes of a far right leader / and his ardent followers
"a hurricane" / a Home Secretary would say
as for the tabloids / I won't even describe
how new terms are coined weekly / to describe us

nobody stops / to think
why we have refugees / in the first place
we run away from wars / rape, stigma and death

here we meet / humiliation
name calling / and utter disrespect
given a choice / none of us would choose
this kind / of life
no rational being / chooses suffering

life is filled with uncertainty / things could change
many of us would turn / into refugees
if Russia was to point its guns / at the UK
instead of Ukraine / if Israel was our neighbour

it is easy to dehumanise / others
when you have unchecked power / and authority

however

proper leadership calls / for an empathetic heart
that feels the pain / of the stateless
the poor / and the vulnerable

as for our friends and allies / you can do something
about this disruption / there is plenty room
for those wanting to / do the right thing
stand up for humanity / be an active ally
work together / and support each other
respond to hateful comments / on Facebook or X
challenge the bigoted ignorant brains / educate them
and show them love / reach out to refugee groups
to show your support / protest with us
like / our local MP does
bring other people in / there is plenty room

for those wanting to / do the right thing
speak up when you see these things / ask always

as for you my brothers and sisters / sanctuary seekers
maybe / we are the real "wretched of the earth"
as mentioned by Frantz Fanon / although our futures have
been shaped / by wars
violent conflict / and other strife
in this environment / let us learn
to be self reliant / most of us are skilled
nurses, engineers and artists / poets and all
let us not sit / on those God-given talents
but exercise them / even if for no money
just to keep sane / in an insane environment
don't allow the depression / and hopelessness we have
carried for a long time / to take us to the grave
on account of not being accepted / or being labelled

may we all remember / refugees are people
be kind to them / most of whom you see
are the only living members / of their bloodline
some have not seen / any loved ones for years
we are just people / don't call us illegal ever again
we are human / caught up in a bad situation

Hungry

thank you to the chicken shop
the one where I bought three chicken strips
my meal for the whole day
nobody reminded me of the drink
that comes as part of the meal
they must have spotted that my spirit was ill
the strips were tasty
eaten in hungry haste
and wrapped in fiery hot chilli
which I would usually not consume
for medical reasons
but who cares!
any hungry tummy wants to be filled
be it that of a king or a pauper

I Was Not Born an Activist

there isn't one perfect single way
of being an activist

it is not a vocation
or a calling
but the primal human response
of anger and outrage
at the injustices being meted out
on other people
and the environment

for that reason
no one is born an activist
I was not born an activist
and there is no training school

activism is an exhibition of passion
and belief
which comes with an active demonstration
of those feelings

there is street activism
characterised by marches
meetings and protests
I am heavily involved in
I have the tools of the trade
banners, T-shirts, placards

and sometimes leaflets
explaining what we are fighting for

impromptu street addresses happen all the time
and during Covid restrictions
a megaphone was a veritable friend
to send out the voice
to the two-metre distanced listeners

it is not restricted to the street
I have been involved in protest theatre too
in which the burden of womanhood
and the injustices of patriarchal and capitalist societies
were the focal points

activism requires a lot of energy
I have travelled the length and breadth of the UK
from attending reading sessions at vigils
outside Birmingham Queen Elizabeth hospital
organised by DocsNotCops
and PatientsNotPassports
to spoken word recitations on top of river Thames
or pickets alongside affected communities

just yesterday
15th October 2023
I was at the #PalestineLivesMatter rally in Coventry
which was part of a global movement
against apartheid infrastructures
in this case built by Israel

some of the meeting invitations
come at the last minute
sometimes I arrive at a protest without knowing
there was one planned

being always prepared is a necessity

I almost always have my placards rolled up nicely
for easy carriage and storage
and I remind friends to charge up batteries
for megaphones
there is often a protest on the go
fuelled with rage and love

as for me
I carry some bit of writing
all the time
I have been asked on so many occasions
to recite a poem
or two

the British government has attempted to criminalise
protests
and encouraged people to perceive activists
as disruptors
of business and normal life

see how
the recent gatherings

blockaded the street near and to
Heathrow airport
against its expansion

the rebels
as they are often called
decidedly sat on the road
to prevent traffic passing
were people who loved their neighbourhood
and wanted to protect its legacy

think about the world we live in
and how it has been shaped by activists
even when it meant
risking their own lives

think also about how hypocritical
it is to condemn activists
and at the same time
praise Nelson Mandela

Martin Luther King
a figure of hatred and fear
is now celebrated every year
for the change he brought in the USA

just for a moment imagine
how long it was going to take women
the right to vote in this country

a selfless death
means that we now vote
just like men

it is easy to take these things for granted
but this is my inspiration

a tiring activity
for many nights of aching feet
are the telltale signs of my fatigue
moments when I could do
with a nice full body massage
and a full roast chicken at Nando's

it doesn't come with remuneration
and we need to look after ourselves
and each other
or else
we are prone to activism burnout

Ubuntu

I am
and you are
and we are

in my culture
no one is left behind
like a line of insects
going home

we are aware
that we are merely
passing through this space

we share it
for a limited time
we share
       our food
       our time and most importantly
       our stories

family structure is made of the eldest
to the youngest

living together
working together
and eating together

using not spoons
but hands
touching each other
in the same plate

nobody gets food poisoning because we all do
nobody gets sick because we all do
nobody just dies because we all just die too
from grief

age is revered
a repository of life experiences
and wisdom cascaded down
one word after another

no one goes to an elderly home
we have one home
our home
that is Ubuntu

because I am
and you are
and we are

Ubuntu
is who I am
and
there is no I
without we

Refuge

I shall sit here until my bum is numb
because this is home
a refuge to me
far away from home
my everything and nothing
given by people
I never get to meet

but I am also aware
that all these places
like the library
need more funding
to keep their doors open
for those like me with not much
but a craving for books
and knowledge

Single Grand

I want you to know
my granddaughter
that I care

I love you

I am sad I cannot be there
to see you
being gifted to the world

I get hurt when I hear your father
saying he misses me
I worry
how will he introduce me
to you?
a woman who abandoned him
when he was 14?

I get confused
during WhatsApp video calls sometimes
with your mum
we have not met
yet
what will she say about me
a woman she waited to see on her lobola day
but never showed up?

day and night
I feel the pain
another layer
added on top

listen
granddaughter
my love comes from as far
and as deep
as an ocean

I am waiting here
with your shoes
your laces
with your clothes and nappies
with your toys
ready to support you

will you forgive me
before you show up?

I want you to be my friend
drive me to the hospital
when I am unwell
bend on our knees together
in prayer
more than anything
I will always be with you
in spirit
when physicality prohibits

Ode to Activist Lawyers

O legal advisers, guides and mentors
who help us navigate
the complex world of the UK asylum
and immigration system

you are the ones who give us direction
who help us understand
the laws and the regulations
and the demands of the land
that we seek to call our own

you are the ones who help us
find our way home

you listen to our stories
hear our dreams
give us hope
offer us options
to make our journey smoother
our path clearer
you are the ones
who help us overcome
fear and anxiety
they call you activist lawyers

you are the ones
who give access

to the future
that we long to see

who give us the tools
to build a life
that is full and free

our immigration advisors
activist lawyers
we thank you
for all that you do
and all that you are

you lead us through
to the land of opportunity
and the life that we desire

you are the ones
who make it all possible
you are the ones
we admire
and acknowledge

Kukaya

phwata! phwata! pitter patter!
thunderous arousal
waking every creature
the gentle sound of rain
accompanied by deafening thunder

that is one of my earliest memory
in grandma's hut
huddled behind her
lying on her reed mat, wulili panji javi
dreaming of a big man in the clouds
pissing on us all
and farting from time to time

rivers and lakes started swelling
and getting angrier
at times claiming lives in their swift gullies
rapids and waves
too strong
even for the strongest swimmers

the lightning was brutal
                              mphamba yawa!
killing people and cattle
huge trees breaking into pieces

the damage
creating enemies
out of ignorant villagers
who accused each other
of causing it
taking away their livestock
and relatives

rain meant plenty

wild fruits shared
by both birds and humans
a garden of Eden
with no one cultivating

benign downpour
nature tendering

in my community
there were rain rituals
the chiefs and Group Village Headmen
would go out to pray
and sacrifice a white sheep
to ancestors and gods
ku Chitendi

the ceremony almost always
led to heavy rains afterwards
which drenched animals
people and fish

old grass thatched huts
bore the brunt
exposed leaky roofs

the soil was not spared
cascades of muddy waters
converged at the lake
their splashing sound
a reminder of Kukaya, home

Investing in Our Future

children are lovely
but sometimes demand too much
when we are already tired from work
or in another mood

children have no idea
that they are being difficult
for them it is all part
of growing up

we need to look at the bigger picture
it shall be over soon
children will grow up
and it does not take long for that to happen
they are changing everyday

their smiles light up our faces
and as we grow older
they too will complain
about us being demanding
and hard work

my son who is now thirty
used to make me feel the same, stressed
but now he is my best friend
the most protective prince
and a father to his own

A Note on Love

family is everything
I come from a large one
with countless children
grannies, aunties and uncles
nephews and nieces
some of whom I don't know
by name
still
we all celebrate because
our genes are the same

I love people
of all ages and background
because my family is exactly like that
varied
with similar values
of respect and kindness

expected behaviour from an elder
and expected behaviour from a child

a silent education
unwritten rules
unspoken chapters
brought into the family
many many years ago

then
I have a larger family
the older I get
the wider my circle of friends

I do not relate with every acquaintance
as my values have to be respected
in the relationship
it is so easy to let other people
take control of one's life
impose toxicity
and I am not going to allow it

all those that I welcome in
must play a positive role
no matter how small

and the groups I relate to have also spiralled
with age
I find myself in so many
poetry, asylum, women, black women
they all make me feel
I belong

I shall always surround myself
with loving people
if they disrespect me
I get out of their life
because I love people
but I love myself even more

Don't Come Back Here

I could hear friends mocking
      hostile gesture
           finger pointing
                whispered accusations
like a witch to be tied to a stake
I had crossed the line

sporting days were better
I could draw into myself
cry, mutter and
go in

there was no hidden sanctuary for my tears
the toilets were too dirty, classrooms too bare

no space in the whole campus
for one girl
who was pregnant

the smell of cabbage from the kitchen
filled me with nausea
but that was the only and last meal
I vomited
in silence

my body was no longer my own
nose bleeds and showers were now one

the sense of taste too sharp
for the gritty campus food

a third eye and ear developed in me
I could hear a conversation tens of metres away
I could sense body language from afar
whispers and gossip flooding me
                              a creature from Mars

then came a nurse
to do a physical pregnancy check
innocently called
by the headteacher
and the Judases in my class

I nearly passed out
as she squeezed and pressed my nipples
harder and harder
until some liquid came out

this was the confirmation

my fate was sealed

soon I was standing in front of the head Sister
"you have been withdrawn due to pregnancy
go and be a mother, not my student
take this letter of dismissal
give it to your guardian, your brother
or whoever!"

"how many months is it?"
she asked
I did not answer

I sauntered away listening to the echoes

"don't come back here!
you're not wanted

don't come back here!
you'll spoil our innocent students

don't come back here!
whatever you do,
don't come back here!"

Have You?

have you supported a stranger
sick, flailing and failing
falling down in the unforgiving grip
of hunger and death?

their gratitude is more than a million words
their radiating smile
a whole world

have you supported a stranger
directed them on the correct path
when they had lost their bearings
stayed with them until they found their place?

their trembling hands
as they wave goodbye tells it all

have you rescued a stranger
who was so burdened
by life's twists and turns
that they had lost the will to live?

the conversation of their unbelieving eyes
speaks volumes bigger than Shakespeare's

have you cheered on a champion
in the throes of ever receding victory

made them realise that they are winners
and this is just a game?

their doubling of energy in an exhausted endeavour
only happens because someone cares

that someone could be you

have you supported a student in need
about to be withdrawn from university
pointed them to the right direction
so they could win a scholarship?

have you supported a friend
about to be swallowed by a big debt
not necessarily through money
but just by saying
"it will be alright"?

spread the love
create magic in the hearts of those drowning

will you?

Thirty-Two

they have always been there

since I have become old
all I do is maintain them
with a toothbrush and toothpaste

funny how lately
the dentist asked me

are all these your teeth?

What If

I have gotten used to living alone
surrounded by books and schedules
filling in the day
weeks and months
with writing and reading

but what if one day
I struggle to breathe
who will take the lead
to undress me
and give me fresh air

I have gotten used to struggle
with my unruly kinky hair
even when I go out
I do it alone
like a lone spider in its lair

I often wonder
who will

reach for my back
help me take off my bra
unfold the layers of flesh
on my rib cage
dry my sweating fingers
and lift up my chest

who will be my partner
when I exercise
and go on brisk walks
to shift the weight
open my lungs
and help me run faster
in pursuit of better health

yes
I need someone
to read my work
a silent editor
not this inanimate teddy bear
whose glassy eyes just stare
I wonder if he cares

yes
I need someone
to compliment
and silently reproach me
as I drool over a piece of cake
it is not easy to lose weight
when living alone
or is it?

Dear Elder Loraine

I am glad you've made it
to eighty years!
your skin is wrinkled
but your spirit is still alive
you still walk with a purpose
and a smile

age has not taken much from you
in fact
it looks like it has brought you grace

look at how
you take things
look at how big
your family has become
grandchildren
and great grandchildren

all these beautiful beings
pointing to you
as their source

I would like to think
you have mellowed
over the years
like mature wine

the potent energy of
writing and speaking
acting and activism
has slowed down too

I am sure you now enjoy sunsets
and wake up late
when it's warmer

your face shows contentment
you do not blame anybody
for anything
nor do you carry any baggage
from the past

you have let it all go
you have learnt the meaning of love
the importance of forgiveness
and voluntary forgetfulness

you deliberately put aside
all the painful memories
that served no purpose

whose photos are these
on the wall?
your friends
in your younger days
at parties

very daring
very loud and
cheeky

photos of many
homeless friends you helped
some dead
some living
some grandparents like you

how about these books?
wow! I can't believe you
wrote more than ten books
of poetry, prose and children's literature

you have really had a blessed long life
and contributed so much
to others and your community

look again at the photos
Malawians in Leeds
daughters of Nyasa dinner and dance parties

surrounded by memories
now you can watch
the flowers grow
and appreciate
a life well lived

you have done well

thank you for living with
a purpose
and that purpose being others

one more thing though
please remember
when you think it's getting darker
and you are about to depart
it will be to another realm
where a new adventure awaits
and life starts all over again

lots of love,

Loraine

Solidarity

I have been exposed
to the love of strangers
seen direct smiles
or smiling faces
under masks

it has been eye-opening

      to know that so much solidarity exists
      in this city

      that a homeless girl can share
      a life and be provided with a home
      away from home

it has been a learning curve

      to have my privileges checked
      closely

      for a Malawian girl to speak
      English and be handed numerous awards

it has been mind-blowing

      to experience greatness
      alongside respected leaders

I have seen

the better side of humanity

love instead of hate

it warms my heart
and gives me hope
that humanity is in a better place
in how it cares for other humans

PART 2

STOP

with an introduction
by Cryton Chikoko

Introduction

Loraine's public campaigns have contributed so much in relieving the plight of many migrants in the UK. This recent addition of her pen to her voice adds more fuel to the fight. Her advocacy against the Home Office's Hostile Environment and racist bordering inspires many of us migrants to stand up against state injustices. Many politicians and news outlets rarely allow the public to see migrants as fellow human beings, rather only as villains. In this section, Loraine powerfully counters the negative publicity surrounding migrants.

What follows are poems that reveal, inspire, educate and rebuke. You will learn that migrants aren't so different from people who haven't migrated. Among other themes, Loraine captures with precision the world of poverty, loneliness, anguish and uncertainty callously set up by the UK government against people seeking refuge in the UK. She warns perpetrators and supporters of the Hostile Environment that "we are all just one conflict away / from being refugees."

In a world where migrants are never allowed to be seen as heroes, blowing our own trumpet is imperative. In "Unsung Heroes," Loraine gives a snippet of the outstanding contributions of migrants worldwide—reciting the vital contributions of black inventors and mentioning some powerful black human rights campaigners. It doesn't escape Loraine that it is hugely the carbon emissions, the plunder of Africa and wars initiated by the Global North that are fuelling migration. In Africa, Western nations bring "huge cargo aeroplanes that bring in guns / and take away precious minerals," she writes. Hopefully, by the end of this section, those who choose to pander to divisive voices, that feed violent stereotypes and ignore the benefits that migrants bring to host nations and the world at large, will be converted. On the other hand, the poetry here will build the resilience of marginalised people held hostage by unfair systems in the West.

Cryton Chikoko

Cryton Chikoko is a migrant.

Keeping Africa Poor

I was born in a Continent
rich with dark earth
and dark people
yet I don't see the wealth
I stepped on
all my life

minerals of rare metals
lie beneath the ground
I pounded with my bare feet
everyday

my dusty village
shaped by gullies and erosions
is now my place of worship
and grief
revered for giving life
to us all
but also watching us die
one by one

we worship the elements
the age-old sun
and the sun god only answers with
  more heat
  hot wind
  and less rain

the endless suffering visited upon my people
and those like me is
unimaginable

the inherited government systems
are all failing
serving their masters in Europe and
keeping Africa poor

I have seen so many
with a skin colour like mine
dark
having collapsed
from the long walks
across the unforgiving desert
or with stomachs bloated
with briny water
after another drowning

this is now daily news
daily deaths

my search for peace too
could have ended up
in the Mediterranean sea
my body admired by mermaids
a soul gone too soon

I stand here
amazed

by how my life has changed
I was charged like a criminal
and have survived
the potential of being a shark's meal

I will still talk on behalf
of those that never made it
knowing that if there is a place
where all the dead converge
one day we shall all
meet

We Are Dying

we are dying
in isolation
alone and forlorn
with not much change
with not much hope
even in death
"they don't matter"

we are dying
no inquest
no investigation
like a useless life
has just gone
no one needs to know

we are dying
our trauma is always downplayed
wars, bullets we witnessed
and abuse flying towards us
have made us feel
       unworthy
       unloved
       and undeserving

we are dying
we leave behind
orphaned children

paralysed by the meaninglessness
of their own lives

everything about us ignored

we are dying
the hand of oppression is heavy
but there's no need for muscles
to lift it off
come   out,   shout!

we are dying
sing their names!
let everyone know
that they too
once walked this earth

we are dying
say their names!
remind the world of
lives   cut   short!
lives that mattered to us

we are dying
beat the drums!
drum the call to a siren!
not to war
but to a new level of consciousness
that says
our lives matter

we are dying
break the silence!

we too are humans
documented or not
spread the message
of love

we are dying

we   are   dying

we   are   dying

Aeroplanes

the people of Ukraine just a few months ago
were busy living
but are now running for safety
like all of us
called refugees

so

      is it their fault?
      are they primitive?
      do they like to fight?

in a strange country
with a different alphabet
unable to even read road signs
they carry only their lives

so

      will it be hate
      or pity?

because at the end of the day
we are all just one conflict away
from being refugees

and we all know what war means
hopelessness is written
on children's faces

some people are lucky
to be born free
others are not

deprived
homeless
sometimes stateless
in a foreign land with no next of kin

so

        will we put a stop to tyranny
        dictatorship and war?

sing

        stop! stop! stop!

no amount of weapons can win
over the burning will of people

the war in Palestine
is likely to last a thousand years
flaring up now and again
with every new generation

and we know
peace cannot be negotiated
by people in tanks or in military aircrafts
but needs equal partners
on the ground
seeking a lasting solution

in the Congo forest right now
makeshift airports exist
where huge cargo aeroplanes bring in guns
and take away precious minerals

imagine if these aeroplanes landed
with hospital or school building materials
and books to educate the young

so we are saying
        stop the war
        stop corporate greed
        and all sing
        STOP! STOP! STOP!

Queueing

being an asylum seeker made me last
always the last one
even if it was for free

I have queued for toilet paper
and less

now my status has been granted
I shall have the front seat
in the housing queue
you kept talking about

after all you said
"asylum seekers get everything easy"
so where is it?

I can't find it
but people ask me
"what have you been doing
since getting your status?"

I would love to answer
"jumped the housing queue"

Seeking Dreams in the Streets

a female friend tells me
"that night
when I reached the door
and found keys left inside the lock
to block me out
I closed my eyes tightly
to make sure I wasn't dreaming
the third eye reached for the hedge
I wasn't afraid of the cold
nor humans

a multitude of snails
with and without shells
licked me everywhere
asking me to open my mouth
sensing I hadn't eaten for days

when I come to your house
please do not serve snails
on the kitchen table"

seeking dreams in the streets
another female friend says to me
"for four days I hadn't had a bath
under the bridge where I lodged
I became aware of my own smell
I now bathe twice a day

when I come to your house
please don't ask me why I love baths so much
I am paranoid that the smell would return"

seeking dreams in the streets
this male friend says in excitement
"the graveyard was the best of all!
no one spat on me
but I realised I couldn't speak
I didn't know if I was alive or not

when I come to your house
please don't shut me off
when I speak"

seeking dreams in the streets
another male friend says
"I was very happy
sleeping in an old car
it was safer than the open space
although I couldn't stretch my legs

when I come to your house
please don't ask me
to drive your car"

seeking dreams in the streets
an elder friend tells me
"the refugee organisation I trusted
handed me a sleeping bag

and led me to my new home
the pavement

when I come to your house
don't let me sit or sleep

on the hard floor"

Christmas

Christ-mass
a mass for Christ
enjoyed in wintry houses
where a fake Santa glides
in the inky sky
bearing children's presents

a fairness of the worst kind
used to condition children
to compete for goodness
before they even know
how to spell
their own names

Christmas
sometimes spelt Xmas
the Christ's day
all made of fake clay
as shopkeepers ululate
and shoppers flood the streets
with trolleys and baskets
buying food they shall not eat
and presents they shall not value

a cacophony of till sounds
with teeming spenders
investing their last pounds and pennies

kwachas and tambalas
to celebrate a wrong date
for a wrong reason

a community so trained
to be top consumers for a day
even religion stands at bay
on 25th December

the endless nights
where children sit
on their windows
staring into the dark
sky
waiting for a sledge
with a big tummy
visiting all the houses
in one night
at the same time

what a waste
and what a crime

We Pray

we pray to connect
with something greater
to discover peace
and find a saviour

we pray to lift our hearts and minds
and to leave behind
the worries and the doubts
that weigh us down

we pray to lift our spirits
and to turn things around
to summon the courage
we need on our way

we pray for those we love
and those we hold dear
we are there for them
through all the joys and all the pains

we pray to ease their strains
to touch their lives
share their burdens
lighten their loads

we pray for many reasons
and in many ways

we pray to find the peace
that comes from grace

we pray to find the strength
to face each day
to find the love
that guides us on our way

Amen

Now I Sing

the cold
at winter vigils
the hoarse voice
from chanting
freedom slogans
at Broadgate Coventry City Square
the jibes and snide looks from "decent" people
confused by all this hullabaloo
I survived it all

I am convinced of two things
I am a fool
who does not know
how to give up
nor to give in
until it all lines up

I cried
wailed
and scratched

holding on
to a life torn apart
by years of living in fear
poverty and anxiety

I was not the only one
some paid the ultimate prize

it crossed my mind too
but the fight was bigger
than my puny life

so I fought
we fought
and covered it all
in prayer and hope

now I sing
with joy and victory
for the success of my case

let it not be forgotten
that many still suffer
with lives in limbo
this fight has come to an end
and begun again

see y'all in your streets

New Policy

the UK government has no shame
once again it is looking for victims to blame

those who run away from persecution
death and destruction are apparently better off
in a land which barely thirty years ago
had an ethnic cleansing genocide that
     raged
     ravaged and
     raved
set huge fires
and left a million ghosts
who are waking up
to another fight of troubled minds
sharing Rwanda
with the estranged
in a land with no recourse

the advert for "Visit Rwanda"
has been taken too far

victims whose lives are in danger
will find their days even stranger

what's wrong with seeking asylum here?

Unsung Heroes

Inspired by Joan Potter's book *African American Firsts: Famous, Little-Known, and Unsung Triumphs of Blacks in America*

whenever we celebrate
Black History Month
we mostly celebrate the fighters
the warriors, the pacifists

we talk about Malcom X, Nelson Mandela
Martin Luther King, Harriet Tubman
black scientific excellence, discoveries
and explorations are left out

is this a deliberate action
forcing us to focus
on the struggle of life
rather than the exploration
of its other beautiful gifts

many people are not
likely to know of Elijah McCoy
yes The Real McCoy
the first automatic lubrication
of machinery

or Frederick Patterson
who created a car
just ahead of Henry Ford

nor the man who came up
with the life-saving
blood transfusion system
Charles Drew
who died of lack of blood himself
after an accident
because hospitals would not take in
a Black dying man

I am not sure we all know
how at thirty-three years old in 1987
Dr. Benjamin Carson
became the first neurosurgeon
to successfully separate twins
joined at the head

he was not the first
miracle healer though for in 1893
Daniel Williams
another Black man
had performed a successful
open heart surgery operation

our Garret Morgan
inventor of the first traffic lights in 1923
now enjoyed all over the world

bringing so much understanding
amongst road users

these are just
some
of the unsung heroes
you should look for
and educate the world on

Another Death Is One Death Too Many

another death is one death too many
it is a tragedy
to see a life cut short
before its time
to see a family torn apart
by the hands of crime

                              we have lost him

another death is one death too many
it is a reminder
that life is not a penny
to be taken lightly
or thrown away
it is a precious gift
that we should cherish
every day

                    she would have wanted to live

another death is one death too many
it is a call to action
to do something
to make a difference
and to stand up tall
to fight for justice
to give it our all

                              he was twenty-three

another death is one death too many
but we cannot let it be
in vain
we can honour the fallen
by standing up
for what is right
and by fighting for a future
that is brighter and brighter
                   his body was frozen from the open window

another death is one death too many
but it doesn't have to be the end
we can come together
and we can make a change
we can create a world
where every life can mend
                   he must have passed three months ago

2022 Malawi Floods

have turned mountains into rivers
houses and cars are learning to swim
as they get abandoned by owners
some gone
some still here

unhoused villagers
relying on the goodwill
of donors
yet
no support
in sight

Coventry Canal

up and down the canal
I gaze at the green cloudy waters
a lizard-like creature crawls
over my feet
before it disappears
in the bush
nearby

first comes a polite cyclist
then a proud dog walker
finally a pulsating runner

a homeless man is sleeping

breathing deeply is all I do
for I can't touch
the freezing waters

I Own Nothing

I have a roof above my head
I am glad
but it belongs to someone else

I have no bills
I am just an occupant
a happy occupant
I own nothing

I don't have to pay
anything
I don't own this space

yes I am happy
but something really bothers me
and breaks my peace
I own nothing

where is home?

I have others paying for me
like a child I have to be looked after

one day I shall hand back my room keys
when my time is up
where do I go from here?
I own nothing

I get anxious
and these thoughts
break my peace

I once had a home
a house I could afford
like the life I once had it's all gone
I own nothing

state-enforced destitution
it is called
I am an asylum seeker
no job, no income, no hope
no rights

I am grateful
for the hand of providence
on my life

yet I fear another hand
which at the stroke of a pen
can take it all away
and just like that
this breaks my peace

what breaks it even more
is that I am not alone
so many are stuck
in this loop

this breaks my peace
I own nothing

this breaks my peace
we own nothing

PART 3

FIGHT NO MORE

with an introduction
by Dr. Moira Dustin

Introduction

It should go without saying that I was honoured by Loraine's invitation to introduce this third part of her new collection. More than that, it gave me the opportunity to step outside of daily life for a brief time and immerse myself in the wondrous world of her poetry and word-power.

Loraine's work is an emotional explosion. The snippets of life she shares with us illustrate all human experience. From the deep sadness and love of "It Was Not Meant to Be", to the dark humour of "I Am Losing It", to the exhilaration of "Good News," the reader is bounced from one experience to another – exactly as we are in everyday life. Loraine endows humdrum experiences with meaning, and allows the reader to experience familiar phenomenons in new ways. But she also has the ability to make the unknown recognisable in ways that illustrate the human connections we all share: I've *sometimes* wondered what the moment of having refugee status recognised is like and now feel I have some small sense of it; I've *never* wondered what it feels like to be a beaten up and weathered old car but now I do, as a way of understanding the toll that the journey to refugee recognition can take on a person. It's no surprise that remedial work is required at the end of that journey—"everything in me needs replacing." Yet despite almost constant movement and transit, we see a deep connection with place. Wherever Loraine is, connections are made, communities develop, warmth and care grow.

What stays with the reader is the sense of the passage of time and the ever-forward movement of a human being through her own life story. We have an understanding of the past that has shaped Loraine as a warrior and a princess, the love for people who are gone but remain alive in her memory (and now in her work), the future that is unknown but awaited with hope. What soul food for the reader.

Moira Dustin, November 2023

Moira Dustin is co-convenor of Women in Refugee Law, a network to centre refugee women in international law, policy and practice.

Good News

you have refugee status!
who, me? are you serious?

I screamed
laughed
and cried at once

engulfed by emotions
alien to me

a question why, why, why
kept pestering
my overwhelmed senses

my mouth shivered
my voice crackled
a buzzing sound came
into my ears
the radio songs I love
stopped making sense

did I lose it?
is this how it feels
to be human?

to be floating in
unspeakable euphoria?

Sound of Silence

I have been listening
I can't hear a thing
except for
a stone of silence
sitting between my ears
covering them from sounds all around
there is no muffle
or whistle or whisper
and I am beginning to love it

my new definition
a life filled
with motion
commotion
brought down by lethargy
and drops in energy
to live in silent thoughts
always listening
but not hearing

The Drive

for the longest time
I have felt like a car
parked outside

I have gotten wet
and rusty overtime
I have absorbed all the heat
from the sun
I have watched my paint crack
and come off

my battery running low
fuel line clogged
looking like I have come to the end
of the line

changing parking spaces
from hotels to hostels
with chained doors

smell of soggy tasteless rice
sensory overload
of negative vibes

I have watched my tyres
get ripped
tired of being tired

at other times
pressure getting too high

I am now finally unparked
ready to be used again
friends fixing me

in the distance
a tune
Hallelujah! Justice has been done

everything in me needs replacing
maybe it's the price
of freedom

I Am Grateful

I am grateful
for the people who lift me up
when I am down

I am thankful
for the air that I breathe and
for all the beauty that I see

look
there is food on my plate
I have shelter too
that keeps me safe at night
from the bite of the crispy wind

I am grateful
for the clothes on my back and
for all the memories
I have had

I am thankful
for moments that bring me joy
happiness and laughter

I am grateful for the sun
and the rain
for the chance to love
and the chance to gain

I am thankful
for the opportunity
to grow
and to learn
and to know

I am grateful
for all that I have
for all that is yet to come and
for every blessing
big and small

I am so grateful for it all

for they all have a role to play
in this game

called life

I Am Losing It

I am losing it
my sight I mean

wearing glasses for the first time
something I always avoided
afraid that lenses will mist
from my tears

the test was
eye-opening
random letters
in fonts so small
even the optician's assistant
could not read them

Visa to Travel

as a migrant
one of the biggest challenge I had
was money

I struggled to get food
and warm clothing in winter

and today
the biggest irony of all
is that my Award sponsoring company
is a global financial player

Double Grand #1

the scar on my left knee
comes from
a childhood accident
in the fields

Grandma stopped all her work
put me on her back
and walked
barefoot for five kilometres
to the nearest hospital

she did not stop
or complain
my welfare was the only thing
on her mind

she could not let her grandchild go
untreated
she was the one feeling the pain

she never left me alone again
I still feel her hand
holding mine with love
wherever I go

Double Grand #2

he was a leader
our loving grandfather
calm, tall and wise
his eyes sparkled
like the stars in the skies

he was the patriarch
of our village
the one
we always held dear

he had a heart
full of love
that glued together his three wives
and his uncountable grandchildren

he had a spirit
that was always above
the troubles and the strife
he was the one
who found a way to sing
through all the trials

he was the one
who left his long foot mark
on footpaths
his name

written all over the forests
of tangerines, mangoes
bananas, guavas and oranges
he grew and preserved

he was the one
who guided us
with his ancestral wisdom
embellished with grace
under the moonlight
and at any time
with his distinct judge's hat

he was the one
who effortlessly chased the lions
mambas
and hyenas
with his walking stick
so we could all see
tomorrow again

our loving grandfather
calm, tall and wise
he was the one
who always
held us together

I Don't Melt

there is a space in me
where no mind or body
exist
nobody can touch me
I need no company at all
I'm alone
and it's alright

all memories lie there
next to me
an undisturbed pile

once in a while I pick up one
and flick through it
then cast it away

in this place
I don't bleed
hate, cry or fear
I am just me

a queen and a warrior
in a kingdom I rule

this is a place I return to
every time
fires start

a place I return to
every time
storms visit

I lock myself in
while on a train
full of people
and watch
through the window
of my soul
inaudible insults
all wash over me
like water
I may be wet
but I don't melt

next time your world speeds up
look in for this place too

for you have it in you

I Am Becoming

my grandmother
I think and act like her
stopping with a load of wood on her head
or a pail of water on her arm
multitasking
and taking everything
in her stride

I now love Berekete dish
as well as walking barefoot
feeling the earth beneath my feet

I can see myself
constantly digging
for this or that
with a headscarf on my head
always thinking of
what to do next
to make sure the family is fed
and children are ready for school

I am becoming my grandmother
supporting kids I am not related to
educating and advising strangers
like I have known them forever
having opinions about
everything
and everyone

I am really becoming her
she who shared all her possessions
and in the end was left with little
if any
but never cared
"you cannot take
anything
beyond the grave"

yes I am becoming my grandma
filled with pride and wisdom
never begging
even if my tummy rumbles with hunger

forever a princess
who faced hills
droughts and famines with a stoic face
"this too shall pass"

I am becoming
my grandmother
knowing
that nothing lasts forever
and that at the end of it all
these majestic mountains
shall one day become
molehills
and she who laughs now
shall cry tomorrow

it is OK
for me to be
my grandmother

Wandering

I have been wandering
from place to place
house to house
since I was eleven

a year later
I embarked on a journey
in search of my mother
in the city
where she lived

my grandfather
gave me
two ripe bananas
and a prayer

my grandmother
tracing my footsteps
kept screaming my name
but I was too determined
to listen
eventually
she gave
the driver
enough
for me to go

I was riding a bus
for the first time
every drop of vomit I captured
in my spare dress
was worth it

a few days later
like a dream
I saw my mother
smiling at me
from the veranda

It Was Not Meant to Be

I wish
I had touched
your small dainty hands
rubbed your smooth stomach
and watched your toothless smile
heard your gurgle talk
and witnessed your first steps

it was not meant to be

and the memory of you shall never end
a bond too deep
to crack

I saw in you
the one I could have handed my baton to
narrating our uneasy walks
    the falls
    the rises
all the tales we could have told

I wanted to touch your little nose
that really looked like mine
and see my reflection
in your clear brown eyes
showing me as a small spec
in a window of my very own soul

we shall never hold you
but in heaven
or whatever place
the dead go to
we shall look out for you
and fulfil these words

Grandson
because we loved you
before you were born
and in death
we love you even more

Light

living in a world
filled with colours and sounds
I am surprised
and mesmerised
by the kaleidoscope
feeding my eyes and ears

I can't hear the ants
move on the grass
next to me
but I can certainly taste the breeze
on the hair
of my arm

I am alive

and I am all of life
brimming with health
and gratitude

in sadness and loss
I forget to see beyond
the cries and whistles of birds
all around
diluting my senses even more
with their watery notes

I forget
that I am the light
that God planted on Earth
to shine and reflect myself
in the pain of others

I have been lost
in the loving looks of elders
whose memories have been washed
by the years
I dive into the energies
they have expended
on us all who are the future

I am that for which without
there is nothing

I am more of everything

Free at Last

to be free at last

to be able to speak and
to live as I wish

to be free from chains and from oppression
to live in a world that grants me expression

to be free at last
to be able to live and
to think and
to do

what we want
without fear
or doubt
or hate

to be able to love and
to shout

to be free at last
to choose our own fate

to be able to rise and
to fly and
to soar

to reach for the stars
and open the door

to be free at last
or so it seems

but the journey is long
and the fight is not done

for freedom is a flame
that must be won

The Last Breath

the goodbye day
when the last breath is breathed
maybe with a dry sigh of surrender
I worry
that things may go wrong

I may not be ready
for the bells when they toll

something tells me though
through His Word
that I shall be ready
like I have been
for everything else
my Creator
has it all planned

it is indeed perfectly human
to want to know the unknown
that one day we must face
that final journey
feared by most

who cares?
like all others before me
I shall move

and maybe wait
in a place where souls congregate
before appearing again
when the time is right
for I believe in deathlessness

I shall not spend my human experience
wondering about it all
for what shall happen
shall happen
and only when it happens

but whilst waiting
    I shall share a smile
        some laughter
           and even some tears
for they too are only for a while
before the cycle starts
all over again

Things to Do When Facing Change

Allow enough time. Digest and absorb. Let it sink in. Sometimes change is the best thing to ever happen to us, although unfamiliar at first.

Balance out your options. The outcome will be based on the one you take.

Count on friends, because they could be holding the keys. Let them support you.

Develop a list of things, a plan. Build your own compass to help you navigate the journey. Unplanned responses lead to unplanned outcomes. Be sharp on this one.

Expel the negativity. Instead, welcome opportunities. Change is the only constant we face in life.

Inject the required amount of energy for best results.

Laugh, always laugh, and enjoy the moment. It really is the best medicine. Most challenges lessen when we laugh at them. You are bigger.

Rise up again and again for the world to see who you really are. As someone said, a strong person falls seven times and wakes up eight. Be that.

I Do Not Want to Fight No More

I am fifty
five decades
scarred
at times scared
a sacred life spent
in personal and collective struggles
a fighter for both
the self and others

I am fifty now
and exhausted
a witness to pain
sorrow, tears and blood
born from a mother who watched
her husband die
as she was pregnant

I am a survivor
strong and alive
having fought malaria
at three months old
and won
little did I know
of all the other battles

I am finally blessed with fine health
a free gift worth more than wealth

and I see my children
play with their own children
and I laugh alone
with anger sometimes
at the madness of life

I hear echoes from my father
who died at thirty-two
the soft voice of my mother
who lost her life at fifty-one
the childish timbre voice of my sister
who left at six
and the deep voice of my brother
who passed away at forty-one

I am fifty
I feel l have arrived
the biggest battles
hopefully
behind me

I now join the village of elders
ready to give counsel
to the new generation

I am fifty
I do not want to fight no more

let me live in peace
for once

hear the laughter
of my newly born granddaughter
as the chirping of night insects
pass through the open window

Closing remarks by Alphonsine Kabagabo

I met Loraine in 2021 when I became the Director of Women for Refugee Women. She was on my interview panel, as one of the organisation's trustees. Little did I know that in addition to being an incredible activist and a voice for the voiceless, she was also a fantastic writer and comedian!

Reading Loraine's first poetry book, *I Was Not Born a Sad Poet*, blew me away. I found it incredibly moving and I have quite a few favourite poems, even if it is hard to choose. For instance, "I Am Enough" reminds us that circumstances shouldn't define who we are...

This second collection from Loraine is just as powerful. I read with excitement all these beautiful poems covering so many varied topics: friendship, solidarity, activism, hope and support, culture, sadness...

Reading "Ubuntu" filled me with joy.

"Ubuntu
is who I am
and
there is no I
without we"

Loraine is a proper example of Ubuntu! If the decision-makers of the UK immigration policy had

"Ubuntu," Loraine and many others would not have to live in limbo for years.

The poems give a good insight into Loraine's life, her childhood, her amazing grandparents, her activism and determination from a very young age. It is humbling to read about Loraine's family, her granddaughter she didn't abandon but had to live away from ("Single Grand"), her culture and memories ("Kukaya"), the shame of teen pregnancy ("Do Not Come Back Here"), death ("We Are Dying"), patriotism ("Keeping Africa Poor"), homelessness ("Seeking Dreams in the Streets"), ... There is more: "Unsung Heroes" is a real history lesson. "I Own Nothing" perfectly describes what it is to be an asylum seeker. "Dear Elder Loraine" is probably one of my favourites. What can I say about the perfect description of Christmas? And yes, she survived it all! And now she sings...

In the third part of the book, Loraine reflects on becoming a refugee, and how such good news comes with mixed feelings. Of course, she talks about the gratitude that we refugees feel for those who understand us.

As Loraine writes in "Light," yes, she is more! She inspires all of us, and is "Free at Last", even if the fight continues...

The more I got to know Loraine, the more impressed I was by her activism, her resilience, her capacity to fight for her rights and above all, the rights of fellow asylum seekers and all marginalised people.

144

I love that Loraine can turn every event of her life into a poem. By now, I am sure you know more about the person she has been.

Whenever you need advice, hope, or inspiration on how to survive and thrive in this Hostile Environment, read this book!

And thank you Loraine for sharing your life with us.

Alphonsine Kabagabo
December 2023

Alphonsine Kabagabo is the Director of Women for Refugee Women, an organisation that supports refugee women and women seeking asylum in the UK to rebuild their lives through empowerment activities and campaigning for a fairer asylum system. As a survivor of the Rwandan genocide against the Tutsi, Alphonsine is one of the few women with lived experience leading an organisation in the refugee and migration sector. She comes to the role after more than twenty years of experience in leadership roles for the World Association of Girl Guides and Scouts as the Director of Africa Region, leading the design and delivery of girl-centred, gender-transformative programmes. Alphonsine is a passionate advocate for girls and women's rights, peace building and cultural understanding. She is a former trustee of SURF, an organisation supporting the survivors of the Rwandan genocide against the Tutsi and a current trustee of Refugee Council, a leading charity working with refugees and people seeking asylum in the UK.

Acknowledgements

I am grateful to everyone who contributed to the publication of *Now I Sing*.

My family who cheer me on and support me in many different ways. Thank you for always believing in me and giving me hope.

Lou Sarabadzic for the total commitment in helping me to develop this book and edit these poems. I encourage you all to visit her website, www.lousarabadzic.com, to know more about her creative writing, translation and copy-editing work. This collection would not be published without her. Thank you from the bottom of my heart.

Tom Green for the technical guidance throughout the process. I never take your support lightly, and deeply appreciate your effort and encouragement in bringing this work to life.

Laura Nyahuye for introducing me to the world of poetry and encouraging me to write. This work would not exist without you.

All the friends who looked at some of these poems and gave feedback, including Mr. Lajabu Makanjila (Mankanj) and Nguni Chief.

My sisters Gloria Adusu, Linda Mlombwa and Molly Mpando for their friendship and generosity, and many others too numerous to mention.

My life coach for seeing my blind spots and guiding me.

Writers at Play and Legacy poetry for the inspiration and support. I always look forward to our Wednesday workshops!

The UK migration sector for all the support I get from performing on big stages to stirring conversations in universities. My friends from Women for Refugee Women, Asylum Support Project (ASAP), Migrants Organise, Refugee Council, Refugee Action, Coventry Asylum and Refugee Action Group (CARAG), Inini Initiative, Status Now 4 All Campaign, Migrant Voice, Baobab Women Project, Stumbling Stones, City of Sanctuary UK, Sing for Change Choir, and all supportive communities in the West Midlands.

Sheila Mosley who helps with the publication and content for my website.

Finally, deep thanks to all collaborators on this project, who despite time constraints, managed to slot me in their schedules, including but not limited to: Alphonsine Kabagabo, Dr. Sue Conlan, Dr. Moira Dustin, Allan Njanji, Grace Manyika, Dr. Rhetta Moran, Cryton Chikoko, Aliya Yule.

Notes

"Failed" was commissioned by Quaker Asylum and Refugee Network for the event "Changing the Conversation on Asylum in the UK," which took place on 16th June 2022.

Earlier versions of "Don't Come Back Here" and "Seeking Dreams in the Streets" appeared in *The Other Side of Hope* online magazine volumes 1 and 2 respectively. *The Other Side of Hope* nominated "Seeking Dreams in the Streets" for the 2024 *Best of the Net Anthology*. Visit www.bestofthenetanthology.com for more information.

Previous versions of the poems "Solidarity," "I Own Nothing" and "We Are Dying" were published in *Hear Our Stories: An Anthology of Writings on Migration*, edited by Teresa Norman, Sinéad Mangan-Mc Hale and Consuelo Rivera-Fuentes (Victorina press, 2023).

The phrase "breaks my peace" in "I Own Nothing" came from an online workshop facilitated by David Dykes from Lyrici Arts in September 2021.

"Keeping Africa Poor" was commissioned in 2023 by *Obsidian: Literature & Arts in the African Diaspora*, a US-based journal from Illinois State University. It will appear in 2024 in an online exhibit.

"Unsung Heroes" was inspired by a book called *African American Firsts: Famous, Little-Known, and Unsung*

Triumphs of Blacks in America, by Joan Potter (Kensington Publishing, 2013).

An earlier version of "I Am Becoming" was published by Legacy Poetry in the anthology *Our Legacy* (2021) by my international creative writing group, Writers At Play, a project run by Legacy Poetry & Equal Arts. Previous versions of "Investing in Our Future," "Now I Sing," "Stranger Friend," and "Things to Do When Facing Change" were published in our anthology *The Art of Letter Writing* (2022).

The poem "Light" was first published in *Common Unity: An Anthology*, edited by NY Writers Coalition (NY Writers Coalition Inc., 2023).

ALSO BY LORAINE MASIYA MPONELA

I Was Not Born a Sad Poet

We live in a world of inequalities perpetuated by capitalism and imperialism. People know poverty and hunger in the midst of plenty.

Loraine experienced it firsthand as an asylum seeker forced to live on the margins of society. This experience moved her to write her first poetry book, *I Was Not Born a Sad Poet*, which has sold over a thousand copies since its publication in October 2022. This book explores the relentless physical and mental exhaustion inflicted by the asylum system. Please check it out here:

Printed in Great Britain
by Amazon

36995683R00088